AUDIT OF THE MANAGEMENT OF FEDERAL PRISON INDUSTRIES AND EFFORTS TO CREATE WORK OPPORTUNITIES FOR FEDERAL INMATES

EXECUTIVE SUMMARY

Federal Prison Industries, Inc. (FPI) is a wholly owned government corporation and inmate reentry program operated within the Federal Bureau of Prisons (BOP) under the trade name "UNICOR." FPI's mission is to employ and provide job skills training to the greatest practicable number of inmates confined within the BOP; contribute to the safety and security of federal correctional facilities by keeping inmates constructively occupied; produce market-quality products and services; operate in a self-sustaining manner; and minimize FPI's impact on private business and labor. In fiscal year (FY) 2011, FPI had $745 million in total sales, mostly to the federal government.[1] The U.S. Department of Defense is FPI's largest customer, accounting for $357 million in sales, or 48 percent of total sales, in FY 2011. As shown in Exhibit 1, FPI's six business groups offer several products and services for sale.

Exhibit 1: FPI Business Group Products

BUSINESS GROUP	PRODUCT EXAMPLES
CLOTHING & TEXTILES	Military apparel, body armor, household items, screen-printing, embroidery services
ELECTRONICS	Braiding and circuit board assemblies, cable assemblies, solar energy, communications
OFFICE FURNITURE	Chairs and seating, desks, tables, filing/storage, accessories, specialty items
INDUSTRIAL PRODUCTS & FLEET SOLUTIONS	Fleet management, prototyping and customization services, storage, fencing, optics and eyewear
RECYCLING	Electronic equipment recycling
SERVICES	Call centers, printing, bindery, data and document conversion

Source: FPI

Because FPI does not receive direct taxpayer funding, it must generate operating revenue to remain a self-sustaining program. However, FPI has struggled financially in recent years, reporting average net losses of $31 million annually from FYs 2009 through 2012 on average net sales of $753 million. FPI's employment figures have also dropped in recent years; as of June 2012, FPI employed 12,394 inmates, or 7 percent of the eligible

---

[1] FPI's FY 2011 total sales of $745 million was comprised of $681 million to federal agencies and $64 million in sales to the private sector as a result of subcontracting, recycling activities, and commercial services.

inmate population, its lowest inmate employment in over 25 years and far below its historical target of 25 percent of the eligible BOP inmate population.

The OIG conducted this audit to determine what factors have led to the significant reduction of inmate work within FPI, and FPI's plans to maintain and create work opportunities for inmates. This audit covers FPI operations from FY 2001 through August 2012.

Results in Brief

We found that FPI's reduction in inmate employment is primarily the result of efforts to compensate for declining revenues and earnings. FPI officials told us that a combination of factors had contributed to its recent financial struggles. Among these are changes to the legal and policy framework in which FPI's businesses operate that were designed to reduce FPI's impact on the private sector, such as new procurement requirements that lessen the impact of FPI's mandatory source authority and new market share thresholds for certain FPI product lines. The officials also cited the winding down of the wars in Iraq and Afghanistan, the U.S. economic downturn during the late 2000s, and substantial financial losses in key product lines as having contributed to the declining overall financial results. To compensate, FPI implemented factory restructuring initiatives in FYs 2009 through 2012 in an attempt to offset ongoing losses, reduce excess production capacity, and reduce staffing as necessary. These cost-reduction initiatives contributed to the loss of approximately 6,500 inmate jobs, or approximately one-third of FPI's total FY 2009 inmate workforce.

While FPI's ability to regain past levels of inmate employment depends primarily on its future business success, FPI has also taken measures to increase inmate employment with existing resources and with the least impact on factory costs. Specifically, FPI implemented an inmate job-sharing initiative intended to employ two inmates on a half-time basis instead of one full-time inmate, thereby introducing more inmates to FPI. However, we were unable to gauge FPI's job-sharing progress over the past 2 years due to a lack of reliable data, as FPI headquarters initially did not provide clear instructions to factory management on how to capture and track the results. Even after clarifying, the resulting performance metric used to measure job-sharing progress produced imprecise results. Furthermore, FPI had not maintained organizational job-sharing targets that would allow it to track progress towards achieving its job-sharing goal, nor had it continually incentivized the achievement of job-sharing success by, for example, incorporating targets and rating criteria into management performance work plans.

Our audit also found that as of June 2012, FPI employed 37 inmates who were under a final order of deportation and therefore appeared to be ineligible for FPI employment under federal regulations. We found that FPI's internal controls did not ensure that aliens who were ordered deported were removed from FPI employment as required. According to FPI officials, as of June 2012, these 37 non-U.S. citizen inmates represented 2 percent of FPI's 1,580 non-citizen inmate employees and less than 1 percent of FPI's 12,394 total inmate employees. FPI officials informed us that once the OIG brought this issue to their attention, they immediately removed 35 of the 37 deportable inmates from FPI employment. Of the remaining two inmates, one claimed he had been misidentified, and one had already ceased working at FPI.

Our report contains detailed information on the full results of our audit, as well as four recommendations to assist FPI in its efforts to maintain and create work opportunities for inmates.

This page intentionally left blank.

AUDIT OF THE MANAGEMENT OF FEDERAL PRISON INDUSTRIES AND EFFORTS TO CREATE WORK OPPORTUNITIES FOR FEDERAL INMATES

TABLE OF CONTENTS

INTRODUCTION

Federal Prison Industries, Inc. (FPI) is a wholly owned government corporation operated within the Federal Bureau of Prisons (BOP) under the trade name "UNICOR." As of June 2012, FPI operated 83 factories staffed by a federal inmate workforce located at federal correctional institutions throughout the United States. FPI inmates produce a variety of products and services, including office furniture; military apparel; communications equipment; vehicle repair and retrofitting; cabinets, lockers and shelving; electronics recycling; and call centers. FPI's mission is to employ and provide job skills training to the greatest practicable number of inmates confined within the BOP; contribute to the safety and security of federal correctional facilities by keeping inmates constructively occupied; provide market-quality products and services; operate in a self-sustaining manner; and minimize FPI's impact on private business and labor.

According to BOP Program Statement 8120.02, *Work Programs for Inmates – FPI*, FPI was designed to allow inmates the opportunity to acquire the knowledge, skills, and work habits that will be useful when released from prison. An additional benefit of FPI is that wages earned by inmates may be used to pay court ordered fines, child support, and restitution. In fiscal year (FY) 2011, FPI reported that inmates contributed approximately $1.6 million of their earnings to these financial obligations. In addition, BOP research suggests that FPI has a positive effect on post release employment and reduces recidivism.[1]

As of June 2012, FPI employed 12,394 inmates, its lowest level of employment since 1986. In contrast, the number of inmates in BOP facilities that are eligible for FPI employment has more than quadrupled from 1986 to 2011. As a result, FPI is currently employing the smallest proportion of the eligible federal inmate population in its more than 75-year history.

Background

FPI was authorized by Congress and created by Executive Order 6917 in 1934 to provide a meaningful work program to inmates in federal penal institutions. To minimize its impact on the private sector, Congress authorized FPI to sell its products only to the federal government, and the Executive Order establishing FPI required it to diversify its product offerings so that no single private industry would bear a disproportionate burden of

---

[1] William G. Saylor and Gerald G. Gaes, *PREP: Training Inmates through Industrial Work Participation, and Vocational and Apprenticeship Instruction,* (U.S. Federal Bureau of Prisons, September 24, 1996).

1

competition. FPI is governed by a Board of Directors, appointed by the President, which is also responsible for balancing the competing interests of operating prison factories while minimizing their impact on the private sector.

Organizational Structure

FPI is a component of the BOP's Industries, Education, and Vocational Training (IE&VT) Division. The Director of the BOP serves as FPI's Chief Executive Officer, and the Assistant Director of IE&VT serves as the corporation's Chief Operating Officer. The Senior Deputy Assistant Director oversees the six business groups, which are each led by a General Manager. See Exhibit 1 for FPI's organizational chart.

**Exhibit 1: Federal Prison Industries Organizational Chart
As of July 2012**

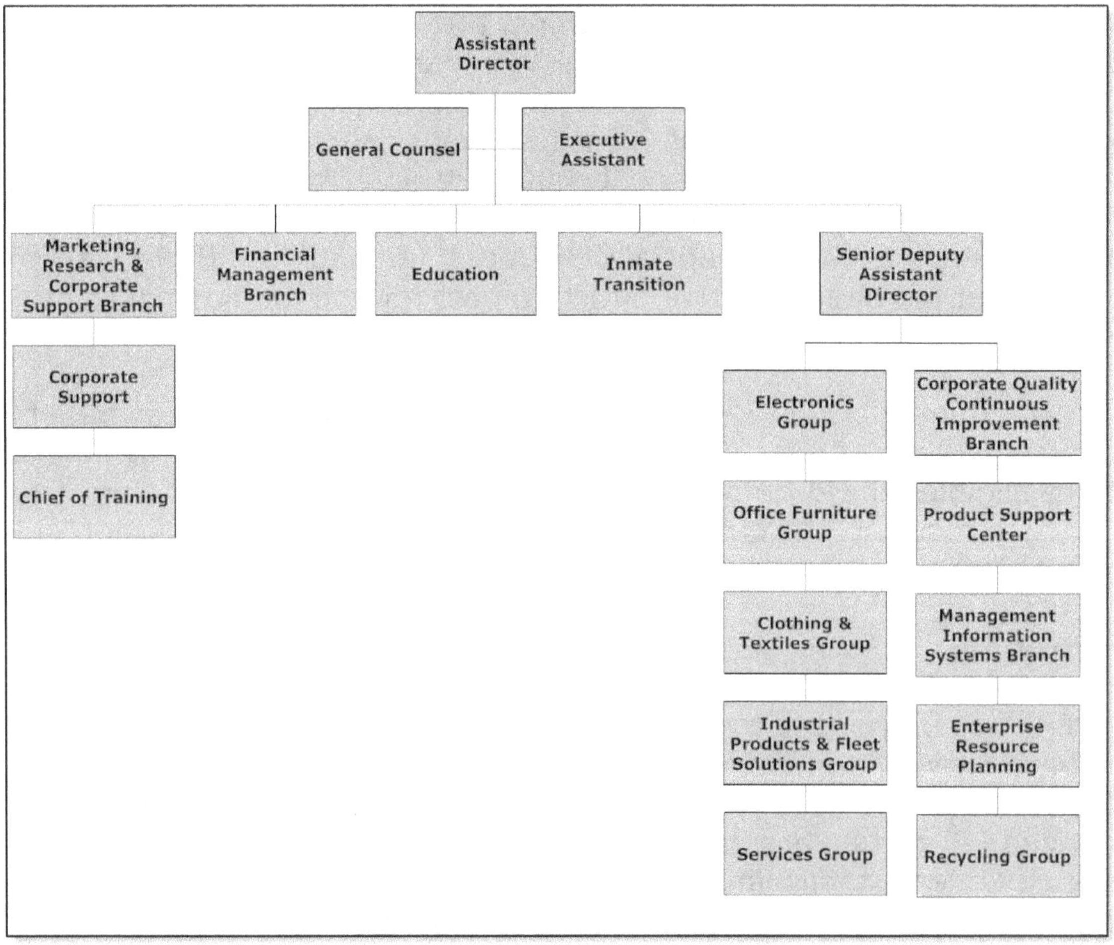

Source: FPI

2

In June 2012, FPI operated 83 factories in 65 prison facilities located throughout the United States. Factories are managed and operated by a Superintendent of Industries, Associate Warden, Operations Manager, or other senior management official; and by civil service personnel who train and supervise inmate employees and provide administrative support. At the end of FY 2011, FPI employed approximately 1,300 full-time, civil service staff.

In accordance with 18 U.S.C. § 4121, FPI is administered by a six member Board of Directors (Board) appointed by the President that represents: (1) Agriculture, (2) Industry, (3) Labor, (4) Retailers and Consumers, (5) the Secretary of Defense, and (6) the Attorney General. The Board is required by 18 U.S.C. § 4122 to provide employment for the greatest number of inmates in the U.S. penal and correctional institutions who are eligible to work as is reasonably possible. The statute also requires the Board to ensure that FPI diversifies its products so that no single private industry bears an undue burden of competition from the products of the prison workshops, and to reduce to a minimum competition with private industry.

The Board's responsibilities also include deciding whether FPI will produce a new product, significantly expand the production of an existing product, or activate a new factory. Additionally, the Board reviews and approves the policies and procedures of the corporation. Board meetings are held throughout the year to discuss the status and financial health of the corporation, changes in inmate population and employment, and any legislative developments or issues.

Product and Service Offerings

FPI offers several products and services for sale to the federal government. FPI's product and service offerings are organized into six business groups, as detailed in Exhibit 2.

Exhibit 2: FPI Business Groups June 2012[2]

Business Group	Product Examples	No. of Factories	No. of Inmates Employed
Clothing & Textiles	Military apparel, body armor, household items, screen-printing, embroidery services	31	4,600
Electronics	Braiding and circuit board assemblies, cable assemblies, solar energy, communications	10	886
Office Furniture	Chairs and seating, desks, tables, filing/storage, accessories, specialty items	10	2,583
Industrial Products & Fleet Solutions	Fleet management, prototyping and customization services, storage, fencing, optics and eyewear	13	1,596
Recycling	Electronic equipment recycling[3]	7	1,145
Services	Call centers, printing, bindery, data and document conversion	12	1,465
Business Group Total		**83**	**12,275**
Central Office Support		**0**	**119**
FPI Total		**83**	**12,394**

Source: FPI

Inmate Employment

Although FPI operates in a business environment, it is primarily a correctional program to prepare inmates for release by helping them acquire job skills and to reduce undesirable idle time during incarceration. All sentenced federal inmates are required to work in some capacity, but not all inmates are employed by FPI.

FPI jobs are in high demand because they offer higher wages than other institutional work assignments, ranging from $0.23 to $1.15 per hour depending on an inmate's skills, qualifications, length of employment, and work performance. Inmates voluntarily apply for employment with FPI and are placed on waiting lists in the order their applications are received. As of March 2010, FPI had 26,335 inmates on employment waiting lists. FPI inmate employees are paid monthly and, after paying a portion toward any

---

[2] Starting in October 2012, the Industrial Products & Fleet Solutions Business Group was discontinued as a standalone group. Its factories were transferred to the Electronics, Office Furniture, and Services business groups.

[3] In October 2010, the OIG issued a report titled, *A Review of Federal Prison Industries' Electronic Waste Recycling Program*. The report describes the results of an OIG investigation into the health, safety, and environmental compliance practices of the FPI's electronic-waste recycling program that identified significant safety and environmental problems with UNICOR's e-waste program, including a failure to implement adequate measures to address the safety of staff and inmates who were employed in the program. It can be viewed online at http://www.justice.gov/oig/reports/BOP/o1010.pdf

court ordered fines or restitution, can use their earnings for such things as purchases at prison commissaries and providing support to their families.

FPI Financial Condition

FPI does not receive any direct taxpayer funding.[4] As a result, it must generate operating revenue to remain a self-sustaining program. From FYs 2001-2012, FPI's net sales ranged from approximately $600 million to $885 million. FPI achieved financial sustainability during FYs 2001-2008, averaging net earnings of $26 million per year. Earnings during this period were primarily attributable to a surge in sales to the Department of Defense (DOD) as a result of the wars in Afghanistan and Iraq, particularly from the Electronics and Clothing & Textiles Business Groups. However, FPI struggled financially from FYs 2009 through 2012, reporting average net losses of $31 million per year on average net sales of $753 million.

FPI officials stated that despite these losses, FPI has remained financially stable due to its factory restructuring and cost containment efforts from FYs 2009 through 2012, as described later in this report. FPI also maintains a capital reserve fund, which contains cash available for short and long-term use and an equipment reserve intended for future capital improvements.[5] The capital reserve fund had a balance of $218 million at the end of FY 2011. FPI's net sales, earnings, and fund balance are shown in Exhibit 3.

---

[4] BOP provides unreimbursed support to FPI in the form of land and certain shared facilities. The notes to the FY 2012 DOJ Annual Financial Statements estimated that the imputed unreimbursed costs of BOP warehouse space used in the production of FPI goods and BOP managerial and operational services provided to FPI was approximately $25 million in each of FYs 2011 and 2012.

[5] A provision of FPI's enabling legislation established the capital reserve fund. All monies under the control of FPI, such as earnings, are deposited into this fund and employed as operating capital for inmate compensation, construction, vocational training and other purposes. See 18 U.S.C. § 4126.

Exhibit 3: FPI Financial Data
FYs 2001 – 2012 (In Millions)

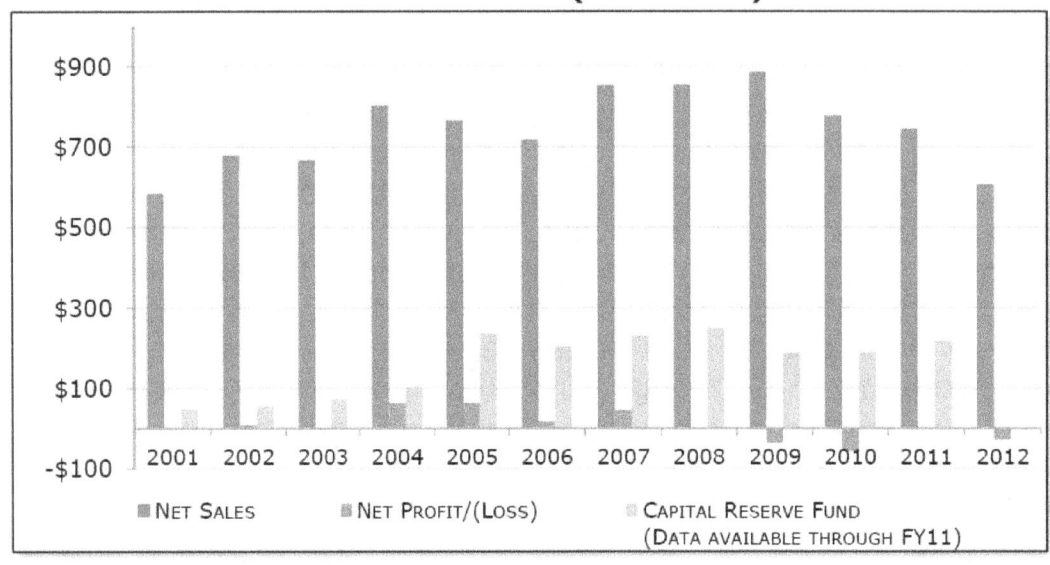

Source: FPI Financial Records

OIG Audit Approach

The purpose of our audit was to determine what factors have led to the significant reduction of inmate work within FPI, and FPI's plans to maintain and create work opportunities for inmates.

This audit covers FPI operations from FYs 2001-2011, but also includes select information through August 2012. To accomplish our audit objectives, we interviewed FPI's former Assistant Director and Senior Deputy Assistant Director, General Managers of its six business groups, other headquarters officials, and the members of FPI's Board of Directors. Additionally, we attended a Board meeting, and we visited six FPI facilities where we interviewed factory managers, observed factory operations, and performed payroll testing.[6] We also examined FPI's data on inmate employment, financial records, and product offerings. Appendix I contains a more detailed description of our audit objectives, scope, and methodology.

---

[6] We performed fieldwork at FPI factories at the following BOP locations: (1) Englewood, Colorado; (2) Florence, Colorado; (3) Tucson, Arizona; (4) Lexington, Kentucky; (5) Loretto, Pennsylvania; and (6) Lewisburg, Pennsylvania.

FINDING AND RECOMMENDATIONS

DECLINE OF INMATE WORK WITHIN FPI AND EFFORTS TO MAINTAIN AND CREATE WORK OPPORTUNITIES FOR FEDERAL INMATES

FPI's ability to increase or maintain inmate employment depends largely on the success of its business operations. FPI's net sales declined 32 percent from FY 2009 through FY 2012, and it incurred a net loss in each of those years. FPI officials attributed the recent struggles to several factors, including changes to the legal and policy framework in which FPI's businesses operate that were designed to reduce FPI's impact on the private sector. The changes include new procurement requirements that lessen the impact of FPI's mandatory source authority, and new market share thresholds for certain FPI product lines. The officials also cited the winding down of the wars in Iraq and Afghanistan; the downturn of the U.S. economy; and substantial financial losses in key product lines.

FPI initiated a job-sharing plan that is designed to increase FPI's inmate employment with existing resources in a revenue-neutral manner, and it decided to prioritize the employment of inmates within 2 years of release. However, we were unable to assess the full impact of FPI's efforts in this regard because its metric to assess its job-sharing outcomes yielded imprecise results. We also found that FPI did not maintain organizational targets for the job-sharing program and goals and incentives for General Managers, which may have limited the effectiveness of its initiative.

In addition, we found that FPI employed only 7 percent of the BOP eligible inmate population at the end of June 2012, which was far below its goal of employing 25 percent of the BOP eligible inmate population. We also found that, as of June 2012, 37 of the approximately 1,580 inmates employed that were not citizens of the United States had been issued final deportation orders and therefore may not have been eligible for FPI employment under federal regulations.

Decline in Inmate Employment

BOP considers FPI to be one of its most important correctional programs because it provides inmates with job skills training, prepares inmates for re-entry into society, improves the safety of correctional facilities, and has been shown to reduce inmate recidivism. However, as of June 2012, FPI employed approximately 12,394 federal inmates, its lowest level of employment since 1986. Moreover, from FY 2007 through June 2012, FPI inmate employment declined 46 percent even though the number of inmates in BOP facilities rose 6 percent. The result is that as of June 30, 2012, FPI employed the lowest percentage of work eligible BOP inmates in its more than 75-year history. Exhibit 4 displays FPI inmate employment since FY 2001.

Exhibit 4: FPI Inmate Employment
FYs 2001 – 2012 (June)[7]

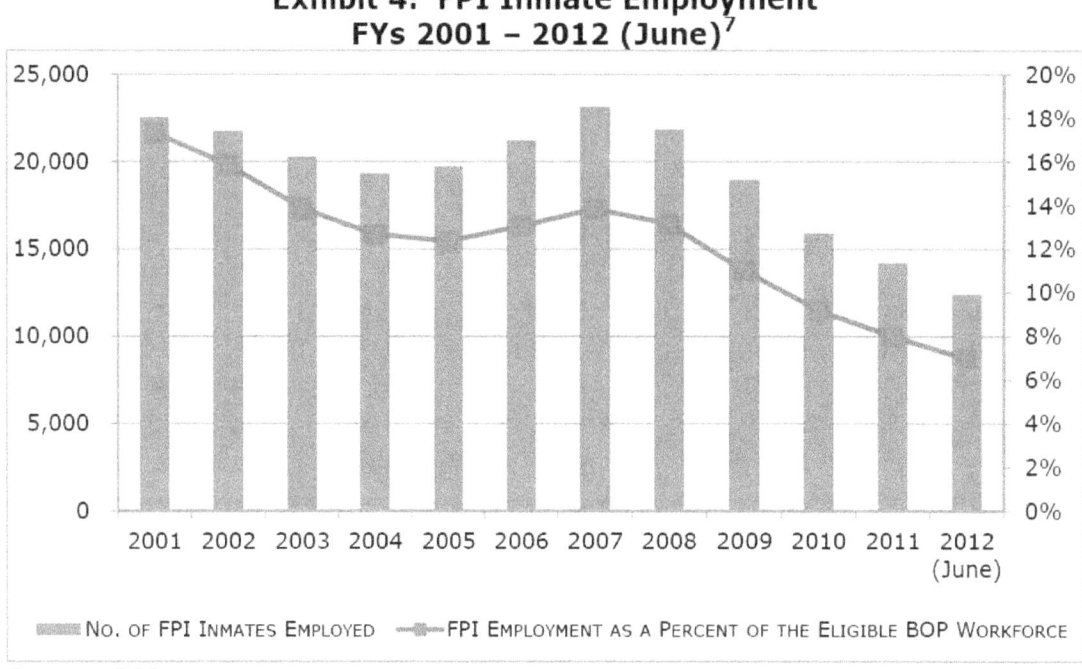

Source: BOP

FPI implemented factory restructuring initiatives in FYs 2009 and 2010 as a cost savings measure to offset ongoing financial losses, and to reduce excess production capacity and staffing to a level consistent with FPI-forecasted business activity. In July 2009, FPI initiated the closure of

---

[7] Near the end of FY 2009, FPI revised its definition of the "eligible BOP workforce" to be more inclusive. To ensure consistency, this exhibit retroactively applies the revised definition back to FY 2001. Further detail on the revised definition is described later in this report.

14 factories and specialized operations and downsized 4 factories, contributing to the elimination of 3,000 jobs between FYs 2009 and 2010. In July 2010, FPI initiated the closure of 9 more factories and downsized personnel at an additional 11 factories, resulting in the loss of 1,700 inmate jobs and displacing 140 FPI civil service employees between FYs 2010 and 2011. In September 2011, in anticipation of a projected $23 million loss for FY 2012, FPI initiated the closure of an additional 11 factories, including its electronics test lab, and downsized 2 factories. Also closed in FY 2012, but not counted as an industrial operation, was the Product Support Center. This restructuring contributed to the elimination of 1,800 more inmate jobs from the end of FY 2011 through June 2012. As shown in Exhibit 5, by June 2012, FPI operated 83 factories, or 21 fewer factories than at the end of FY 2007. Only the Clothing & Textiles Business Group operated more factories in June 2012 than at the end of FY 2007.

Exhibit 5: Number of FPI Factories, by Business Group FYs 2007- 2012 (June)[8]

BUSINESS GROUP	# OF FACTORIES (SEPT. 2007)	FACTORY OPENINGS	FACTORY CLOSURES	# OF FACTORIES (JUNE 2012)
Services	22	4	(14)	12
Industrial Products & Fleet Solutions	20	2	(9)	13
Electronics	12	4	(6)	10
Office Furniture	13	2	(5)	10
Recycling	8	0	(1)	7
Clothing & Textiles	29	5	(3)	31
TOTALS	104	17	(38)	83

Source: FPI

From FY 2007 to June 2012, the Services Business Group closed the most factories. Of its 14 factory closures, 6 were call centers. According to FPI officials, the Services Business Group's call center market declined due to a variety of factors, including rapidly declining sales on a significant contract and legislative and Board limitations on inmates handling personal or financial information. Consumer shifts toward other, often automated and free, options for directory assistance, and towards the use of smartphones, also contributed to the decline. The General Manager of the Services Business Group told the OIG that FPI will eventually phase out its factories providing directory assistance.

---

[8] Factory openings include operations converted from one business group and/or product line to another. Similarly, converted factories were included in factory closures.

The Industrial Products & Fleet Solutions Business Group closed nine factories and during FY 2013 will be discontinued as a standalone group, with its remaining factories transferred to the Electronics, Office Furniture, and Services Business Groups. The Electronics Business Group, which closed six factories since FY 2007, has struggled with excess capacity in its factories, a decline in military orders, and significant losses due to its solar panel and helmet product lines, which are described later in this report.

As shown in Exhibit 6, from FY 2007 through June 2012, inmate employment declined in five of the six business groups, with the exception being the Recycling Business Group.

Exhibit 6: Business Group Inmate Employment FYs 2007 - 2012 (June)[9]

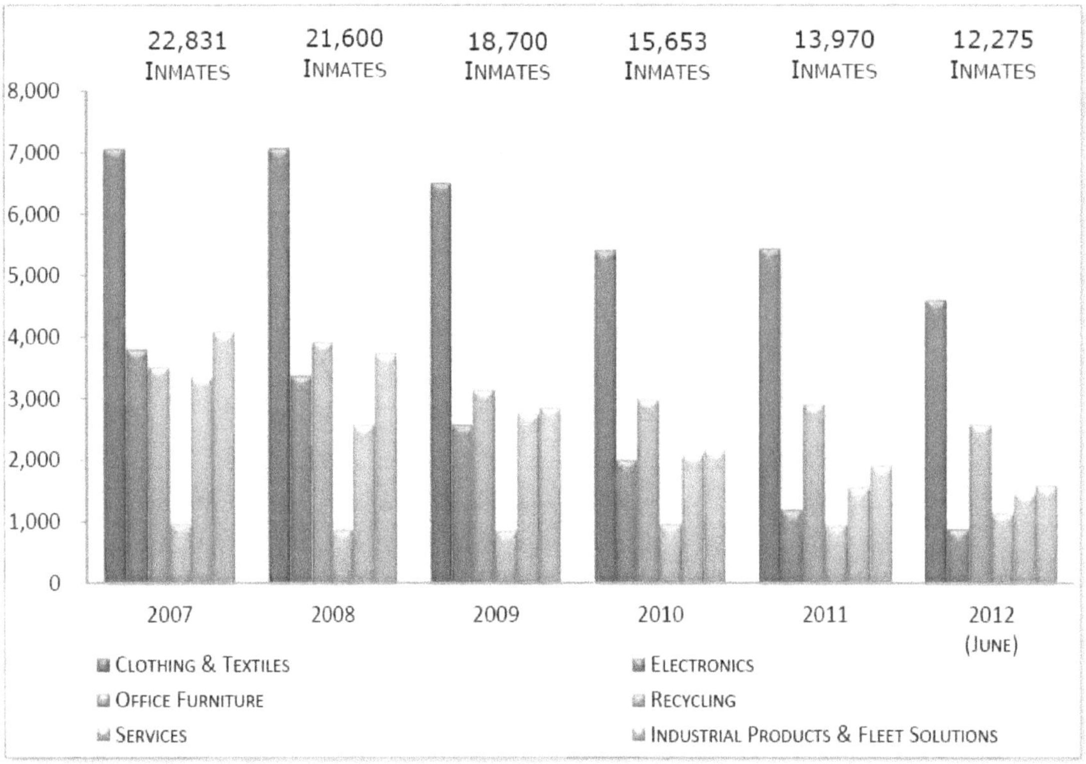

Source: FPI

The Services, Industrial Products & Fleet Solutions, and Electronics Business Groups experienced the largest declines, with each reducing inmate employment by more than 50 percent since FY 2007.

---

[9] Exhibit 6 does not include the small number of FPI inmate support staff. From FYs 2007 through June 2012, FPI employed between 119 and 321 inmate support staff annually.

In addition to the aforementioned reasons, FPI officials said the key factors contributing to the sustained decline in inmate employment were legislative changes and, to a lesser extent, policy resolutions adopted by the Board of Directors that established boundaries on how FPI may operate; the decline in the U.S. war efforts in Iraq and Afghanistan, which reduced demand for FPI products and services; the downturn of the U.S. economy during the late 2000s, which had the same effect; and substantial financial losses in key product lines. The following sections discuss each of these factors in more detail.

Legislative Changes and Board of Directors Resolutions

According to the Congressional Research Service, the "FPI did not face legislative changes from its inception in 1934 to 1988. However, over the past few decades, the erosion of the nation's manufacturing sector, and the increase in the federal inmate population, at the same time the federal government was downsizing, increased congressional interest in FPI."[10] In the last decade, several legislative changes have affected FPI's business operations, as have certain resolutions adopted by the FPI Board of Directors.

<u>Legislative Changes</u>

The most significant legislative changes have involved the modification of FPI's "mandatory source" authority, a provision of FPI's enabling legislation that required all federal agencies to purchase products marketed by FPI instead of soliciting bids from commercial entities.[11] Mandatory source authority has long been highly controversial, with critics asserting that the provision gives FPI an unfair competitive advantage over the private sector that displaces U.S. workers from their jobs. Supporters, including members of the FPI's senior leadership, have historically maintained that the mandatory source authority is necessary to maintain a constant flow of work for inmates.

Legislative changes over the past decade have generally sought to reduce the impact of FPI's mandatory source authority on the private sector. For example:

---

[10] Congressional Research Service, *Federal Prison Industries* (December 8, 2011), 9.

[11] Federal agencies consist of both DOD and civilian agencies, including the Department of Justice.

- **The National Defense Authorization Act for FY 2002** required market research be performed by the DOD before purchasing from FPI and applied to purchases initiated on or after October 1, 2001.

- **The Bob Stump National Defense Authorization Act for FY 2003** modified some of the market research language and established rules stating that the DOD not purchase FPI products or services unless a Contracting Officer determines the product or service is comparable to those of the private sector.

- **The Consolidated Appropriations Act, 2004** stated that for FY 2004, appropriated funds under this act should not be expended for the purchase of an FPI product or service unless the agency making such purchase determines that the product or service provides the best value to the buying agency. This act essentially applied the procedures, standards and limitations of the abovementioned National Defense Authorization acts to civilian agencies for FY 2004.

- **The Consolidated Appropriations Act, 2005** contained language identical to the prior year but now applied to FY 2005 and each fiscal year thereafter.

- **The National Defense Authorization Act for FY 2008** introduced the concept of "significant market share," removing FPI's mandatory source authority if its share of the DOD market for a category of products is greater than 5 percent. This law required the Secretary of Defense to publish a list of product categories for which FPI's share of the DOD market is greater than 5 percent, based on the most recent fiscal year data available.

The National Defense Authorization Acts for FYs 2002 and 2003 and the Consolidated Appropriations Acts for FYs 2004 and 2005 contained provisions, still in effect today, that placed new conditions on when FPI must be considered a mandatory source for products and services. These acts stated that FPI was no longer a mandatory source for the DOD and civilian federal agencies unless the agency Contracting Officer determines that FPI products were comparable in price, quality, and time of delivery to products in the commercial marketplace. If FPI's product is determined to be not comparable on one or more of these factors, FPI must bid against private sector suppliers for the contract under competitive contracting procedures that direct Contracting Officers to select a supplier based on the "best value" to the federal government. Moreover, even if the Contracting Officer determines FPI's product to be comparable on all three factors, the Contracting Officer may nevertheless request a waiver from FPI to purchase the private sector product based on factors other than price, quality, or timeliness of delivery.[12] According to the former Director of the BOP, this legislation primarily affected the Office Furniture Business Group, whose sales declined 44 percent from FYs 2002 through 2007. As a result of these sales decreases, FPI removed approximately 1,780 inmate employees from the program during this period. Since FY 2007, Office Furniture Business Group sales have generally risen but at the end of FY 2011 remain about 29 percent below its FY 2002 sales.

In addition, provisions of the National Defense Authorization Act for FY 2008 that are still in effect established a "significant market share" limit of 5 percent on FPI's sales to DOD for individual Federal Supply Classes (FSC), above which FPI loses its mandatory source authority on DOD sales for these FSCs.[13] As required by this law, DOD must identify and publish a list of all such FSCs, and for these FSCs, DOD can only purchase FPI products using competitive procurement procedures.[14] From the passage of the National Defense Authorization Act for FY 2008 through April 2010, the DOD identified 15 of FPI's approximately 100 FSCs sold to the DOD that exceeded the 5 percent threshold, including 6 of FPI's bestselling FSCs which together accounted for approximately 63 percent of sales to the DOD over the previous decade.[15] Of these 15 FSCs, 11 experienced declining sales in the first year after being listed. For example, the DOD identified FSC 5975, "Electrical Hardware and Supplies," on its list of products exceeding the market share threshold in March 2008 and that FSC remained on the DOD's list until April 2010. From FYs 2008 through 2010, FPI sales in this product category plummeted from $39.9 million to just $376,000. We note, however, that there is no precise method to calculate the direct dollar impact of the 5 percent threshold on a product category's sales, and that several other factors may have contributed to these results, including the loss of a

---

[12] In some circumstances, purchase from FPI is not mandatory and a waiver is not required, including when purchases are made on a competitive basis, public exigency requires immediate delivery or performance, suitable used or excess supplies are available, or the supplies are acquired and used outside the United States.

[13] FSCs are used to group products with respect to their physical or performance characteristics.

[14] If the DOD subsequently determines that the FPI's market share for an affected FSC has dropped back below the 5-percent threshold, FPI regains its mandatory source authority for that FSC.

[15] The six product categories, by FSC, are: (1) 8415 – Clothing, Special Purpose; (2) 7110 – Office Furniture; (3) 8470 – Armor, Personal; (4) 5995 – Cable, Cord, and Wire Assemblies; (5) 6150 – Miscellaneous Electrical Power/Distribution Equipment; and (6) 5975 – Electrical Hardware and Supplies.

significant contract, decreased spending by the DOD in a particular product category, and the effects of other previously mentioned legislation.

In FPI officials' view, the primary effect of the mandatory source authority is now to provide visibility to FPI products by requiring that Contracting Officers consider FPI's products prior to initiating competitive procurement procedures, and allowing FPI to submit bids for competitively awarded contracts.

Board of Directors Resolutions

In 2003, FPI's Board of Directors, which is required by statute to provide employment for the greatest number of inmates while simultaneously minimizing competition with private industry, enacted two resolutions with a direct impact on sales.[16] These resolutions required FPI to eliminate the mandatory source authority for: (1) FSCs with a greater than 20 percent share of the federal market; and (2) purchases under $2,500.[17] Prior to passage of these resolutions, federal agencies were required in such instances to purchase FPI's mandatory source-designated products unless the purchasing agency obtained a waiver from FPI or determined that the FPI's product was not comparable in price, quality, and time of delivery.

FPI officials told the OIG that in the first few years after implementing the 20 percent market share resolution, the greatest impact was on FPI's Cable, Cord and Wire Assemblies product line, for which sales decreased over $20 million from FYs 2005 through 2006. FPI estimated that the Board resolution eliminating mandatory source authority for purchases under $2,500 had a negative net impact of $6.5 million annually. FPI officials could not determine, however, to what extent the declines in sales were also attributable to other factors.

Decline in War Efforts

The DOD is the largest government purchaser of contract goods and services, having spent $374 billion in FY 2011 and accounting for approximately 70 percent of all federal contract sales. The DOD has also

---

[16] One Board member we interviewed described the Board's competing responsibilities of increasing inmate employment while minimizing competition with private industry as a "daily tension."

[17] These resolutions are still in effect today, with modifications: in April 2007, the $2,500 dollar-value purchase threshold was increased to $3,000; and in March 2008, the National Defense Authorization Act for FY 2008 changed the market share threshold, with respect to the DOD, from 20 percent to 5 percent.

been FPI's largest customer, representing 57 percent of FPI's average annual sales from 2001 to 2011, and 48 percent of FPI's sales in FY 2011. In comparison, FPI's next two largest federal agency customers, the Department of Homeland Security and the General Services Administration, accounted for just 21 percent and 5 percent of FPI's FY 2011 sales, respectively. Exhibit 7 shows the breakdown of FPI's sales by agency in 2011.

Exhibit 7: FY 2011 FPI Sales by Customer[18]

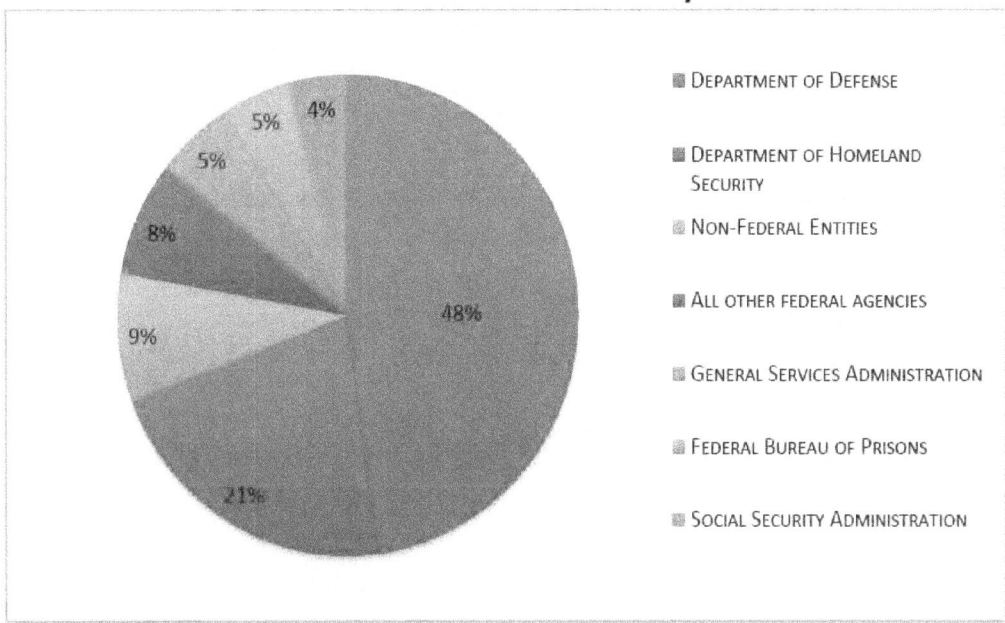

Source: FPI

However, as shown in Exhibit 8, FPI sales to the DOD declined from a peak of $536 million in FY 2007 to $357 million in FY 2011.

---

[18] Differences in totals are due to rounding (the sum of individual numbers prior to rounding may differ from the sum of the individual numbers rounded).

Exhibit 8: FPI Annual Sales to DOD FYs 2001-2011

FISCAL YEAR	TOTAL SALES (IN MILLIONS)	DOD SALES (IN MILLIONS)	% OF TOTAL SALES
2001	$584	$388	66%
2002	$679	$412	61%
2003	$667	$379	57%
2004	$803	$502	63%
2005	$765	$482	63%
2006	$718	$412	57%
2007	$853	$536	63%
2008	$854	$452	53%
2009	$885	$461	52%
2010	$777	$362	47%
2011	$745	$357	48%

Source: FPI

FPI officials attributed this decline mainly to the scaling back of the war efforts in Iraq and Afghanistan; the tightening of the domestic economy, which resulted in increased competition from new businesses that had not previously sought DOD contracts; and as previously mentioned, the legislative restrictions placed on FPI's use of its mandatory source authority when FPI's DOD-related market share exceeded 5 percent on certain products.

Financial Losses to Key Product Lines

Some of FPI's financial struggles and declining employment numbers have been the result of substantial losses to key product lines, most notably the Electronics Business Group's solar panel and military helmet product lines.

In FY 2008, FPI decided to enter into the solar panel market to capitalize on the increased global demand for solar panels and Congressional mandates to increase the federal government's renewable energy usage. FPI's Board of Directors approved the production of solar panels in April 2008, and shortly thereafter, FPI began production at its Otisville, New York facility with an initial annual capacity of 24 megawatts. In May 2009, FPI's Board approved a second solar panel factory in Sheridan, Oregon, to provide geographic diversification and reduce transportation costs of finished panels to west coast customers. The Sheridan factory added an additional 50 megawatts of capacity, bringing FPI's total annual solar panel production capacity to 74 megawatts. However, FPI officials told us that their initial projections of the market for solar panels never materialized because of an unanticipated drop in the market price for solar panel equipment, and that

FPI's efforts to compete in the solar panel market were frustrated by delays in obtaining the necessary certifications showing that FPI solar panels met industry standards for safety and reliability. As a result, in FY 2010, FPI recognized $17.3 million in losses due to writing down the book value of solar cells and panel inventory to market value.

FPI also sustained losses to its military helmet product line. In December 2009, the DOJ OIG initiated an investigation related to FPI's manufacture of military helmets based on allegations that some of the helmets did not meet contract specifications or had failed ballistic testing. FPI decided to waive the mandatory source requirements on the helmets and later suspended helmet production in Beaumont, Texas. FPI subsequently recognized $17.8 million in losses due to writing off the book value of military helmets in FY 2010 and closed its Beaumont factory in FY 2011. As of July 2013, the investigation is still ongoing.

FPI Efforts to Maintain and Create Work Opportunities for Federal Inmates

FPI's ability to maintain and create inmate employment opportunities depends largely on the success of its business operations. In recent years, negative economic and legislative forces have resulted in decreased sales and the FPI's lowest level of inmate employment in over 25 years. These conditions have led FPI to pursue new business development opportunities and new methods to maximize FPI's inmate employment with existing resources. In this section, we describe FPI's recent inmate employment initiatives and business development efforts aimed at maintaining and creating work opportunities for federal inmates.

Revenue-neutral Inmate Employment Initiatives

FPI has undertaken two initiatives to maximize inmate employment in a revenue-neutral manner and re-focus its employment mission. The first initiative seeks to maximize the number of inmates exposed to the benefits of working for FPI through the use of expanded half-time employment, or "job-sharing." The second initiative seeks to expose more inmates with release dates within 2 years to FPI work opportunities. Both initiatives went into effect in September 2010.

FPI Inmate Job-sharing Initiative

In a September 2010 memorandum to all FPI Associate Wardens and Superintendents of Industries, FPI's Chief Operating Officer stated that one method to increase inmate employment is through use of job-sharing, by which two inmates each work half-time to fill a single full time position. This initiative was intended to increase the number of inmate workers employed by FPI while minimizing the impact on factory efficiency and costs.

FPI's job-sharing results appeared to demonstrate that the job-sharing initiative had increased the percentage of FPI's workforce working half-time from 12 percent at the end of September 2011 to 19 percent by the end of the June 2012. However, an OIG review of these statistics determined that the data collected from factories for these results was unreliable. When FPI headquarters compiled its job-sharing results, it expected that factories would count the number of half-time inmate employees, defined as those inmates working approximately 50 percent of a normal factory workweek. However, FPI officials indicated that some factories instead used a BOP payroll definition of "part-time," which counted all inmates working less than 90 percent of the normal factory workweek. This confusion was due to FPI headquarters not clearly explaining to factories how to define and count half-time inmate employees. As a result, FPI job-sharing data collected from September 2010 through March 2012 was inaccurate and, in some instances, overstated. FPI took immediate action upon learning of the inaccuracies by addressing Associate Wardens at all field locations on the intent of the initiative and issuing additional guidance on how factories should count half-time employees.

In addition to this data reliability issue, we believe FPI's method of tracking job-sharing results does not adequately capture the true impact of the job-sharing initiative. As previously stated, the purpose of the job-sharing initiative was to use two inmates, each working half-time, to fill a single full time position, thereby increasing the number of inmate workers exposed to the program. Yet FPI tracks the initiative's progress by reporting the percentage of inmates working half-time without regard to the circumstances that led to the half-time schedule. As a consequence, FPI counts all half-time inmates towards the success of the job-sharing initiative, not just those inmates who are working half-time as a result of the initiative. This methodology risks counting inmates whose half-time schedule is due to other factors, such as inmates who work at a factory that operated half-shifts prior to the job-sharing initiative, or inmates who have had their hours cut due to declining workload instead of for job-sharing purposes. In these instances, since the inmate is working half-time would not indicate that an additional inmate was provided a new employment opportunity with FPI.

The FPI's methodology also does not account for instances where inmate employee work hours are affected by "call-outs," which are scheduled appointments for medical, education, or other purposes that are not included in an inmate's labor hours. Under the FPI's current methodology, inmates with a significant amount of call-out hours could be considered half-time and thereby counted towards the success of FPI's job-sharing initiative even though there may be no direct evidence that additional inmates were exposed to the program. For example, at Federal Correctional Institution (FCI) Lewisburg's Recycling Factory (LERC), participating in the job-sharing initiative was impossible because all available inmates were already working for FPI and there were no additional inmates available to hire. Nevertheless, LERC reported 58 percent of its inmates as "half-time" due to call-outs that reduced inmates' labor hours for the period, and those inmates were included in FPI's job-sharing statistics even though LERC had not actually exposed any new inmates to FPI.

Furthermore, there was uncertainty as to whether a rise in the percent of half-time employment was due to job-sharing success, or the result of a changing mix of full- and half-time employees resulting from reduced workloads and the idling or closing of factories. For example, one factory went from reporting zero employees working half-time in the first quarter of FY 2012 to over 120 in the third quarter of FY 2012. However, during this period, aggregate inmate employment *declined* by 36 inmates, indicating that the increased number of half-time workers did not result in a corresponding increase in FPI inmate employment. The General Manager of that business group told the OIG that when the factory submitted its job-sharing data to FPI, the factory was unable to differentiate actual job-sharing results from the effects of the reduced workload that the factory experienced in the third quarter of FY 2012. We believe that if job-sharing continues to be a priority, FPI should consider a more direct approach to quantifying its job-sharing results, such as counting both the number of inmates hired into a half-time position and inmates whose shifts were converted from full to half-time for job-sharing purposes.

Moreover, data reliability issues notwithstanding, there are indications that FPI's job-sharing initiative may be falling short. Nearly 2 years after the initiative's implementation, approximately 33 percent of FPI's factories had reported zero half-time employees, and in June 2012, the Industrial Products & Fleet Solutions group reported that only 5 percent of its workforce was designated half-time, a significantly smaller percentage than the other business groups. These results may in part be attributable to a lack of incentives for achieving job-sharing results. Specifically, after FY 2011, FPI eliminated job-sharing performance measures and rating criteria from

General Managers' performance work plans because a senior FPI official believed business groups had made enough progress on the job-sharing initiative that the measures were no longer necessary. As of June 2012, FPI had not re-established an organizational job-sharing target that would allow it to track progress towards achieving its goal.

<u>Prioritization of Employing Inmates Close to Release</u>

FPI's Corporate Strategic Plan for FYs 2011-2013 established a strategic goal of increasing efforts to expose inmates with release dates within 2 years to FPI work opportunities. The initiative, formalized in September 2010, was the result of an FPI survey indicating that most inmates were being released without having participated in the program.

To execute this initiative, factory managers were instructed to update factory waiting lists to prioritize the hiring of inmates within 2 years of release, as practicable. Previously, factories hired on a first come, first served basis from a general waiting list, or based on waiting list priority considerations.[19] Although this initiative became effective in September 2010, FPI officials told the OIG that they only began tracking this data around August 2012 at which time 2,795 of FPI's 12,469 inmate employees, or 22 percent, had less than 2 years remaining on their sentence.[20]

During fieldwork at an FPI factory in June 2012, FPI factory management expressed concerns over increased employee turnover associated with giving priority to inmates within 2 years of release, including increased training and other replacement costs, and reduced factory productivity. FPI's Senior Deputy Assistant Director acknowledged these obstacles, but said that they would not prevent FPI from pursuing the initiative, noting that while it is important for FPI to remain efficient and competitive, FPI also must employ as many inmates close to release as possible.

---

[19] Waiting list priority considerations are granted in the case of a factory closing or relocating and displacing an inmate employee; an inmate with a prior FPI work assignment; on a needed skills basis; or for special needs such as participation in the Inmate Financial Responsibility Program, to assist in paying a significant financial obligations, such as restitution.

[20] The number of inmates employed at FPI within 2 years of release as of August 2012 is presented as contextual information only. The OIG has not audited the information because it did not materially support any findings, conclusions, or recommendations. FPI officials told us that the data was obtained from a query of the SENTRY Inmate Management System, which in our opinion is the best available source for this data.

Business Development Efforts

In addition to its revenue-neutral efforts to increase inmate employment, FPI has also undertaken business development initiatives to boost revenue and create new jobs. Two notable initiatives attempt to take advantage of provisions in the Consolidated and Further Continuing Appropriations Act for 2012 that created new opportunities for FPI. First, the Act granted FPI the authority to repatriate, or bring back to the United States, the manufacture of products which are currently, or would otherwise be, manufactured, produced, mined, or assembled outside the United States. Second, it allowed FPI to participate in the Prison Industry Enhancement (PIE) Certification Program, which allows the formation of a joint venture with private industry to produce goods for sale outside of the federal government. FPI's progress toward implementing these initiatives is described below.

<u>Repatriation Authority</u>

FPI officials told us that they were moving aggressively to take advantage of new opportunities to offer products commercially which are currently, or would otherwise be, manufactured, produced, mined, or assembled outside the United States. According to FPI officials, this new opportunity, known as "repatriation authority," creates the potential for FPI to earn significant revenue by either manufacturing and selling repatriated products to the commercial market, or entering into a partnership with a private company where FPI would manufacture the repatriated product and the private company would be responsible for marketing and sales.

As of February 2012, FPI's Board of Directors had approved several pilot projects under its repatriation authority. One such project was the production of photovoltaic solar panels, for which FPI has changed its business plan from marketing solely to federal agencies – the strategy that led to the negative financial results described above – to a pilot project seeking to access the commercial market by providing manufacturing for a partner company that would otherwise manufacture its products outside the U.S. In August 2012, FPI told us that they had met with potential partner companies but had not yet obtained any partnership agreements. FPI officials attributed this to the fact that the overall solar market in general has not improved, and that many companies are reluctant to be associated with the use of inmate labor.

FPI officials also told us that other business groups have been exploring opportunities to use repatriation authority, but since the authority was fairly new, these projects were still in the planning phase. Three such projects were the production of parkas for a textile manufacturer, the production of light emitting diodes (LED) lighting for a partner distribution company, and the production of tents and sidewalls, all of which would otherwise be manufactured or assembled outside the United States. Yet at the time of our audit, FPI officials told the OIG that, in general, repatriation has been less successful than expected, primarily due to unanticipated difficulties identifying domestic business partners willing to associate with the use of inmate labor.

PIE Certification Program

The PIE Certification Program was created in 1979 by Congress to encourage employment opportunities for prisoners that approximate private sector work opportunities. The program exempts certified prison facilities from normal restrictions on the sale of prisoner made goods in interstate commerce, and is designed to place inmates in a realistic work environment, pay them the prevailing local wage for similar work, and enable them to acquire marketable skills to increase their potential for successful rehabilitation and meaningful employment when they are released. Previously, participation in the PIE Certification was restricted to non-federal prison facilities, but the Consolidated and Further Continuing Appropriations Act for 2012 removed this restriction, allowing FPI to seek certification for federal prison facilities under the PIE Certification Program for the production of goods for sale outside of the federal government.

FPI officials told us that they viewed PIE as a less viable option for new business development than the repatriation authority. Specifically, FPI officials told the OIG that under PIE, FPI would be required to pay inmates higher wages, thus increasing overhead costs. They also expressed their concern that, although FPI has received umbrella approval to participate in PIE, each project would have to be individually certified, a process that FPI officials viewed as resource intensive. Additionally, FPI officials told us that based on their assessment of various state programs currently operating under PIE and the variability of market rate wages in each state, FPI was unlikely to be able to pursue regional or nationwide programs, but instead might have to identify smaller, niche markets to be successful. As of August 2012, FPI was evaluating potential business opportunities under the PIE program in light of these concerns, and was in the process of obtaining PIE certification.

FPI's Approach to Business Development

Our audit identified two issues that we believe have the potential to hinder FPI's ongoing initiatives to take advantage of its new business opportunities. First, FPI's former Chief Operating Officer told us that in response to an increase in the number of private sector competitors and to statutory changes to FPI's mandatory source authority, FPI has had to increase its sales and marketing efforts. Yet we found that FPI has had limited experience in sales and marketing due to its previous reliance on the use of the mandatory source authority. Responsibility for business development has been partially transferred to the business groups, and those business groups have taken very different approaches to their sales and marketing efforts. Second, some General Managers of FPI's business groups expressed concern to the OIG that FPI's current business development approach, which relies heavily on the General Managers, negatively affected their ability to oversee the operation and productivity of FPI's factories.

FPI operates a two tiered business development approach. At the corporate level, FPI's Marketing, Research and Corporate Support Branch (MRACS) is generally responsible for outreach and increasing awareness of FPI as a whole, in addition to performing market analysis to comply with the statutory requirements for new product introduction.[21] At the business group level, each business group is responsible for its own product-specific sales and marketing efforts. Consequently, business development efforts to identify new products, markets, and customers have been assigned to the General Managers of each business group with the rationale that each business group would be the most knowledgeable on the products being manufactured and would therefore be in the best position to implement a product-specific business development approach.

Our audit found that FPI's business groups approached their business development responsibilities in very different manners, with some business groups hiring consulting firms and contract sales forces to identify new target markets, and other groups depending exclusively on their existing program managers to identify and develop new products for the needs of their current customers. In addition, many of the FPI officials representing the various business groups told us that their business development responsibilities distracted them from their other operational duties, such as managing the production and order fulfillment processes, and that, as a result, they had to rely on MRACS for business development support even though this function was outside of MRACS's scope of responsibilities.

---

[21] 18 U.S.C. § 4122 (2012)

In August 2012, FPI formed a new business development group at the corporate level. This group was established to pursue opportunities for the growth of FPI's business in all product and service areas, including new business from repatriation and PIE authorities.

Inmate Employment Goal

The Department of Justice embraces the concept of performance-based management, which is the principle that improved performance is attained by focusing on mission, agreeing on goals and objectives and the timely reporting of results. DOJ's Strategic Plan provides the Department's overarching goals and objectives, and DOJ components, including FPI, use this framework to establish their program goals and objectives, implement the programs, monitor performance, and evaluate results.

FPI has a programmatic goal of employing 25 percent of the eligible BOP inmate population. FPI calculates its progress towards achieving this goal by dividing the number of FPI inmate employees by the "eligible BOP inmate population." Prior to November 2009, the eligible BOP inmate population was defined as the number of BOP inmates housed in non-contract minimum, low, medium, and high security facilities where FPI had existing operations, and as a result did not include most male minimum security facilities or detention centers. However, in November 2009, FPI revised this definition to include inmates housed in all non-contract BOP facilities. FPI believed this revised definition was a more appropriate representation of the eligible inmate population. As a result of FPI's change to this more inclusive definition, the percent of the eligible BOP inmate population employed dropped substantially: at the end of FY 2009, FPI employed 11 percent of the eligible BOP inmate population instead of the 16 percent it would have attained under the prior definition.[22]

Despite this change, FPI kept its goal of employing 25 percent of the eligible BOP inmate population. Using FPI's current, revised definition of "eligible BOP inmate population," FPI has not met its 25 percent goal since 1989, when it employed 27 percent of the inmate population.[23] Since FY 2001, FPI employed no greater than 17 percent of the eligible BOP

---

[22] To ensure the consistency of our analyses, and unless otherwise noted, the OIG has retroactively applied FPI's current, revised definition throughout this report when discussing the percentage of the eligible BOP inmate population that FPI employs.

[23] Under FPI's prior definition of "eligible BOP inmate population" FPI last met its 25 percent goal in 2001 when it employed 25 percent of the eligible BOP inmate population.

inmate population, and as of June 2012, employed only 7 percent, the lowest percentage in its over 75-year history. Moreover, while the federal inmate population has steadily grown, FPI inmate employment has steadily decreased; from 2001 through June 2012, the eligible BOP inmate population increased by 47,092 inmates, or 36 percent, yet FPI's employment has decreased by 10,166 inmates, or 45 percent. Exhibit 9 displays the average number of FPI inmate workers as a percentage of the eligible population since 1970 using the current, revised FPI definition of the eligible BOP inmate population.

Exhibit 9: Average FPI Inmate Workers and Eligible Inmate Population, FYs 1970 – 2012 (June)[24]

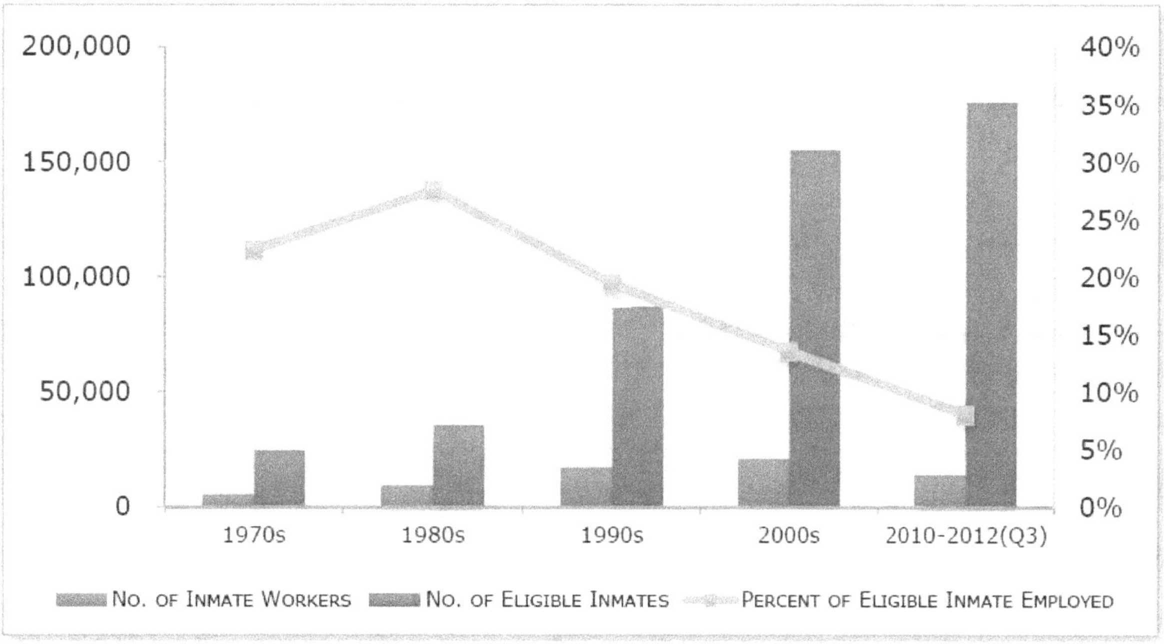

Source: FPI

To have met its 25-percent employment goal for June 2012, FPI would have needed to provide work for over 44,000 inmates, roughly three times as many inmates as FPI actually employed in June 2012, and nearly double the highest employment level ever achieved by FPI. FPI officials told the OIG that due to the continued rise in the eligible inmate population and the more inclusive definition of the eligible BOP inmate population, the 25-percent employment goal is no longer representative of current conditions. Therefore, as of September 2012, FPI was developing a proposal to replace its current employment goal that would be consistent with the Department's commitment to performance-based management and

---

[24] The information in Exhibit 9 is comprised of the average inmate employment, by decade, from FYs 1970 – 2009, and the average inmate employment for FYs 2010 – June 2012.

reflective of FPI's available resources and evolving operational and economic environment.

Employment of Non-U.S. Citizens

Federal regulations prohibit FPI from employing any inmate who is currently under an order of deportation, exclusion, or removal, and direct that any inmate who is currently under an order of deportation, exclusion, or removal shall, unless otherwise excepted, be removed from any FPI work assignment and reassigned to a non-FPI work assignment for which the inmate is eligible.[25] According to BOP Program Statement 8120.02, *Work Programs for Inmates – FPI*, inmates with a deportation order who are appealing the decision also are ineligible for FPI work assignments.

As of June 2012, FPI employed 1,580 inmates that were not citizens of the United States, representing approximately 13 percent of its workforce. Based on BOP information, we found that 37 of these 1,580 non-U.S. citizen inmates had been issued final removal orders by Immigration and Customs Enforcement (ICE) or the Executive Office for Immigration Review and were eligible for deportation.[26] We determined that several of these inmates had continued to work for FPI years after receiving a final deportation order, or had been hired into FPI while already under an order of deportation. FPI's hiring and continued employment of inmates that were ordered deported by a federal immigration judge indicates that it does not have adequate internal control processes in place to ensure that once inmates receive final orders of deportation, they are no longer eligible for hire at FPI or are removed from existing FPI employment.

FPI officials informed us that since we brought this issue to their attention, they have removed 35 of the 37 identified inmates from FPI employment. One inmate continued to work for FPI because he claimed he had been misidentified; FPI is working with ICE on the resolution of his status. One inmate had already ceased working for FPI.[27]

---

[25] 28 C.F.R. §§ 345.35, 345.42 (2012)

[26] This determination was based on a query of the BOP's SENTRY information system focused on inmates designated as "IHP CMPWDI" and "IHP CMPWDE," which means an assessment by the Immigrations and Customs Enforcement (ICE) or Executive Office for Immigration Review was complete and the inmate was, or is to be, deported.

[27] Inmates with a removal order may not actually be removed from the United States in certain instances, such as when the designated country of removal will not accept his or her return. In such an instance, this inmate would be eligible for FPI employment. We identified 9 such inmates during the course of our audit work that were not included in 37 deportable inmates discussed in our report.

Conclusion

Due to its recent struggles, FPI is facing its lowest inmate employment in over 25 years. Although its ability to increase inmate employment depends largely on the success of its business operations, FPI must also pursue opportunities to maximize inmate employment with current resources. We found that, to address this issue, FPI had begun to prioritize the employment of inmates within two years of their release dates, and had implemented a job-sharing initiative to increase inmate employment with existing resources. However, we also found that improvements are needed to ensure accurate and reliable reporting of its job-sharing results, and to establish organizational targets and ensure that responsible officials have appropriate incentives for achieving them.

In addition, we found that FPI's target employment goal of 25 percent of the total inmate population was no longer representative of current conditions due both to the continued rise in the eligible inmate population and to the use of a more inclusive definition of the eligible BOP inmate population. Finally, although federal regulations prohibit FPI employment of deportable aliens unless otherwise specifically excepted, we found that FPI employed 37 inmates that had been issued final deportation orders, indicating a weakness in the FPI's internal controls.

Recommendations

We recommend that FPI:

1. Adjust the performance metric for its job-sharing initiative so that it more directly quantifies FPI's efforts to employ more inmates.

2. Establish organization-wide or business group targets for the job-sharing initiative, and reestablish performance metrics for responsible officials' performance work plans to incentivize meeting those targets.

3. Finalize a policy to replace its previous inmate employment goal with one that is better aligned with the FPI's current operational and economic environment.

4.   Establish internal control procedures to ensure that it no longer considers for hire or employs aliens who have received a final order of deportation, exclusion, or removal, when doing so is prohibited by law, regulation, or policy.

STATEMENT ON INTERNAL CONTROLS

As required by the *Government Auditing Standards*, we tested, as appropriate, internal controls significant within the context of our audit objectives. A deficiency in an internal control exists when the design or operation of a control does not allow management or employees, in the normal course of performing their assigned functions, to timely prevent or detect: (1) impairments to the effectiveness and efficiency of operations, (2) misstatements in financial or performance information, or (3) violations of laws and regulations. Our evaluation of the Federal Prison Industries' (FPI) internal controls was *not* made for the purpose of providing assurance on its internal control structure as a whole. FPI's management is responsible for the establishment and maintenance of internal controls.

As noted in the Finding and Recommendations section of this report, we identified deficiencies in FPI's internal controls that are significant within the context of the audit objectives and based upon the audit work performed that we believe adversely affect FPI's ability to ensure that inmates or detainees currently under an order of deportation, exclusion, or removal are excluded from FPI employment pursuant to 28 C.F.R. § 345.35 (2012). According to BOP Program Statement 8120.02, *Work Programs for Inmates – FPI*, upon receiving documentation that an inmate has been issued a removal order, FPI is required to reassign that inmate to a non-FPI work assignment or removed from the FPI factory's waiting list. However, we found that despite these policies, as of June 2012, 37 of the 1,580 non-U.S. citizen inmate employees had been issued final removal orders by the Immigration and Customs Enforcement Executive Office for Immigration Review and were eligible for deportation.

Because we are not expressing an opinion on FPI's internal control structure as a whole, this statement is intended solely for the information and use of the auditee. This restriction is not intended to limit the distribution of this report, which is a matter of public record.

STATEMENT ON COMPLIANCE
WITH LAWS AND REGULATIONS

According to generally accepted government auditing standards, auditors should identify the laws and regulations that are significant within the context of the audit objectives and assess the risk that violations of those laws and regulations could occur. As noted in the Finding and Recommendations section of this report, we found that FPI did not comply with regulations regarding the assignment of inmates to FPI. Specifically, 28 C.F.R. § 345.35 (2012), states that an inmate or detainee may be considered for assignment with FPI unless the inmate or detainee is currently under an order of deportation, exclusion, or removal. FPI had guidance on the actions necessary to ensure FPI does not employ inmates issued final deportation orders. However, this guidance was not consistently followed. This matter is discussed in detail in the body of this report.

OBJECTIVE, SCOPE, AND METHODOLOGY

Objective

The objective of our audit was to determine what factors have led to the significant reduction of inmate work within the Federal Prison Industries (FPI), and FPI's plans to maintain and create work opportunities for inmates.

Scope and Methodology

We conducted this performance audit in accordance with generally accepted government auditing standards. Those standards require that we plan and perform the audit to obtain sufficient, appropriate evidence to provide a reasonable basis for our finding and conclusions based on our audit objectives. We believe that the evidence obtained provides a reasonable basis for our finding and conclusions based on our audit objectives.

Our audit generally covered, but was not limited to, FPI operations from fiscal years (FY) 2001 through 2011, but also includes select information through August 2012. To accomplish our audit objective we: (1) interviewed FPI's former Chief Operating Officer and Senior Deputy Assistant Director, General Managers of its six business groups, other headquarters officials, and the members of FPI's Board of Directors; (2) attended a Board of Directors meeting in January 2012; (3) visited six FPI factories located in Englewood, Colorado; Florence, Colorado; Lexington, Kentucky; Lewisburg, Pennsylvania; Loretto, Pennsylvania; and Tucson, Arizona; where we interviewed factory managers, observed factory operations and performed payroll testing; (4) reviewed internal controls related to reporting of inmate employment, and (5) obtained and analyzed relevant FPI documentation.

FPI Factory Site Selection

We selected factories from two business groups, Recycling and Electronics, to gain an understanding of FPI factory operations in general. These two business groups were judgmentally selected because electronics was responsible for the highest amount of loss, and recycling is a relatively new business group that employed a large number of inmates relative to its sales. We selected Florence and Englewood, Colorado, as preliminary sites, and then judgmentally selected four additional factories based on the profitability, inmate employment, and product offerings considerations described below.

For each of electronics and recycling factories operating at the end of FY 2011, we calculated the gross profit margin for FYs 2009 through 2011 based on data provided by the FPI.[28] In addition, we calculated the number of inmates employed in each factory per $1 million of factory sales as reported by FPI. The results of our calculations are shown in Exhibit 1 below.

Exhibit 1: Electronics and Recycling Average Factory Inmate Employment and Gross Margin

FACTORY NAME	AVERAGE PROFIT MARGIN	AVERAGE INMATE EMPLOYMENT (PER $1 MILLION IN SALES)
	FY 09-11	FY 09-11
ELECTRONICS		
Danbury Cable, CT	12%	8
Fairton Cable, NJ	-2%	19
Lompoc Cable, CA	8%	15
Loretto Cable, PA	-9%	23
Lexington Cable, KY	12%	26
Marion Cable, IL	-27%	80
Memphis Cable, TN	12%	9
Phoenix Cable, AZ	7%	18
RECYCLING		
Atwater Recycling, CA	-9%	95
Fort Dix Recycling, NJ	23%	59
Lewisburg Recycling, PA	52%	47
Leavenworth Recycling, KS	33%	71
Marianna Recycling, FL	27%	76
Texarkana Recycling, TX	-7%	98
Tucson Recycling, AZ	-20%	92

Source: FPI

Among recycling factories, Lewisburg recycling was selected because it had the highest average profit margin for FYs 2009 through 2011 but the

---

[28] Gross margin was calculated as the average gross profit divided by the average net sales, and represents the average percentage of each sales dollar that is contributed to the profit of the factory. For example a gross margin of 50 percent means that for every $1 in sales, $0.50 is contributed to profit on average.

lowest average inmate employment per $1 million dollars in sales. Tucson was selected because it had the lowest average profit margin for FYs 2009 through 2011 but the third highest average inmate employment per $1 million dollars in sales. For the electronics factories we selected only cable factories for site visits so that we could compare and contrast factories producing similar products.[29] Among the electronics factories analyzed, Loretto was selected because it had the lowest average profit margin for FYs 2009 through 2011 but the second highest average inmate employment per $1 million dollars in sales among cable factories.[30] Lexington cable was selected because it had both the highest average profit margin and average inmate employment per $1 million dollars in sales among cable factories.

Reliability of FPI Inmate Employment Data

FPI provided us with inmate employment data for each factory from its information system. We performed limited testing on this data to determine if this computer generated data was sufficiently reliable for determining the total number of inmates FPI had employed.

To perform our assessment, we reviewed the internal controls over inmate payroll and reporting, and compared SAP reported inmate employment numbers to source documentation for judgmentally selected sample of inmate employees at each of the four factories selected above (Lexington, Lewisburg, Loretto, and Tucson). Each factory records all inmate employees on the door check sheet. At the beginning of each shift, FPI officials record the employees that are present for each shift as well as any inmate call outs that may occur during the day. Inmates may be called out for such things as education classes or medical appointments. At the end of each day, the total hours worked and total calls out hours are tallied on the door check sheets. The sheets are then verified by the factory manager and sent to an inmate payroll clerk for entry into the Inmate Payroll System (IPS). Once entered into IPS, the factory manager will verify that the hours in IPS match the original door check sheets. Following verification, the inmate hours are sent to FPI headquarters for payment. FPI headquarters records the total hours worked from IPS as a lump sum payroll

---

[29] Three non-cable Electronics business group factories were excluded from our site selection analysis: McKean Plastics, Englewood Test Lab, and Sheridan Panels.

[30] Marion cable factory was excluded from our site selection due to its lack of history and losses that appeared to be related to startup costs from operations. Marion cable was first opened in FY 2007, and had its first year of profitability in FY 2011. In FY 2011, Marion cable's profit margin was 25.65 percent. Additionally, FPI officials informed us that Otisville cable was converted to manufacture solar panels, and was therefore excluded from site selection.

expense in SAP, and subsequently transfers monthly inmate payroll to each institution for distribution into inmate accounts.

Our testing compared the payroll data in IPS from a judgmentally selected sample of 10 inmate employees for June and September 2010 and 2011 to the door check sheets. We found the sample data contained within IPS matched the data recorded on the door check sheets. Additionally, we compared the inmate employee data in IPS to the data provided by FPI from the SAP system, and found that the data was sufficiently reliable for the purposes of our audit.

During our testing of the data we did identify one limitation of the inmate employment data that was significant within the context of our audit. FPI officials informed us that inmate employment data is reported to headquarters on a quarterly basis, but the inmate employment data from SAP provided to the OIG reported the number of inmate employees as of the last day of each fiscal year. Therefore, FPI's employment data does not capture all inmates that may have worked for FPI from October 1 through September 29 of each fiscal year. We compared inmate employment for September 2010 and 2011 to inmate employment for June 2010 and 2011 at each of the four factories where we performed testing, and did not identify any changes in inmate employment of greater than 1 percent. Therefore, despite this data limitation, we did not identify any significant variation in inmate employment over the tested pay periods that would lead to an incorrect or unintentional conclusion on the number of inmates employed by FPI.

FEDERAL BUREAU OF PRISONS'
RESPONSE TO THE DRAFT REPORT

U.S. Department of Justice

Federal Bureau of Prisons

Office of the Director   Washington, D.C. 20534

September 3, 2013

MEMORANDUM FOR RAYMOND J. BEAUDET
                ASSISTANT INSPECTOR GENERAL
                  FOR AUDIT
                OFFICE OF THE INSPECTOR GENERAL

FROM: Charles E. Samuels, Jr.
                Director
                Federal Bureau of Prisons

SUBJECT: Response to the Office of Inspector General's (OIG)
                DRAFT Report: Audit of the Management of Federal
                Prison Industries and Efforts to Create Work
                Opportunities for Federal Inmates

The Bureau of Prisons (BOP) appreciates the opportunity to respond
to the open recommendations from the draft report entitled Audit of
the Management of Federal Prison Industries and Efforts to Create
Work Opportunities for Federal Inmates.

Please find the Bureau's response to the recommendations below:

Recommendation 1: Adjust the performance metric for its job-sharing
initiative so that it more directly quantifies FPI's efforts to
employ more inmates.

BOP's Response: To advance this objective, FPI has provided
guidance to the field, tightening its parameters on the definition
of part-time employment for purposes of its job-sharing initiative.

with the ultimate goal of increasing work opportunities for inmates. This has been done through nationwide communications with our field leadership and follow-up written guidance distributed electronically to all field locations. The FPI will reissue guidance at its upcoming management teleconference. Accordingly, we request that this recommendation be closed.

Recommendation 2: Establish organization-wide or business group targets for the job-sharing initiative, and reestablish performance metrics for responsible officials' performance work plans to incentivize meeting those targets.

BOP's Response: As demonstrated in the graph below, FPI continues to make excellent progress with this initiative. This progress has been the result of continual emphasis on the importance of this initiative through nationwide video conferences, teleconferences, and the issuance of written guidance. In addition, this is tracked through the agency's Strategic Plan, as well as through quarterly and monthly reporting.

Percent of Part-time Inmates

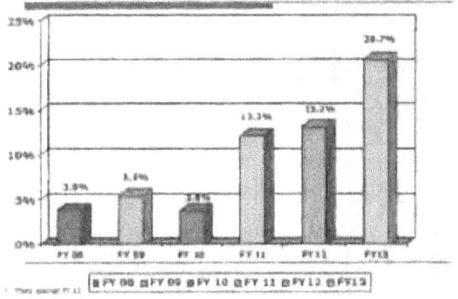

Although no longer included in the performance work plans, the data confirms that excellent progress has been made in increasing the number of inmates participating in job-sharing by 20 percent, which exceeds the number for FY 2013; this is a 57 percent improvement from the prior year. For these reasons, we request that this recommendation be closed.

2

Percentages in the above bar chart are as follows. FY08: 3.9%, FY09: 5.5%, FY10: 3.8%, FY11: 12.2%, FY12: 13.2%, and FY13 (third quarter): 20.7%.

Recommendation 3: Finalize a policy to replace its previous inmate employment goal with one that is better aligned with the FPI's current operational and economic environment.

BOP's Response: We do not concur that changes to the inmate employment goal should be made at this time. Specifically, by capitalizing on its new repatriation and Prison Industry Enhancement Certification Program authorities and implementation of employment initiatives, including job-sharing and hiring prioritization, FPI believes it can make significant strides toward reaching its current employment goal. We have achieved this goal in the past and do not want to lower our desired goal and expectations for the future. Accordingly, we request that this recommendation be closed.

Recommendation 4: Establish internal control procedures to ensure that it no longer considers for hire or employs aliens who have received a final order of deportation, exclusion, or removal, when doing so is prohibited by law, regulation, or policy.

BOP's Response: FPI is currently in compliance with Program Statement 8120.02, CH 3, p 4, 5(a); and 28 CFR § 345.35(a). We have confirmed that the only inmates working for FPI who have received a final deportation order are those who qualify for a policy exception, and cannot be removed from the U.S. because the designated country of removal will not allow them to return. FPI has provided the field with guidance on BOP/FPI policy in Program Statement 8120.02, and intends to remind managers of this requirement during the next management video conference. Additionally, this information will be included in the monthly operational reports for all factories. Accordingly, we request that this recommendation be closed.

If you have any questions regarding this response, please contact Sara M. Revell, Assistant Director, Program Review Division, at (202) 353-2302.

3

OFFICE OF THE INSPECTOR GENERAL
ANALYSIS AND SUMMARY OF ACTIONS
NECESSARY TO CLOSE THE REPORT

The OIG provided a draft of this audit report to the Federal Bureau of Prisons (BOP). BOP's response is incorporated in Appendix II of this final report. BOP did not concur with one of the OIG's four recommendations and did not explicitly state whether it concurred with the other three, resulting in all four recommendations being unresolved. The following provides the OIG's analysis of the response and a summary of actions necessary to close each recommendation.

Recommendation Number:

1.   **Unresolved.** BOP did not state whether it concurred with our recommendation that FPI adjust the performance metric for its job-sharing initiative so that it more directly quantifies FPI's efforts to employ more inmates. BOP stated in its response that to advance this initiative, FPI has communicated with and provided follow-up written guidance to all field locations, tightening its parameters on the definition of part-time employment for purposes of its job-sharing initiative, with the ultimate goal of increasing work opportunities for inmates. BOP also stated that FPI will reissue guidance at an upcoming management teleconference.

   BOP's response provided little detail about the contents of FPI's guidance or whether it addressed our concerns about FPI's performance metric for the job-sharing initiative. Among those concerns, which are documented on pages 18-19 of this report, are our findings that the data collected from factories to quantify this initiative's results were unreliable, and that FPI's methodology for computing its results does not adequately account for half-time employees or for instances where inmate employee work hours are affected by call-outs.

   Accordingly, to resolve and close this recommendation, please provide evidence regarding the adjustment of the job-sharing performance metric, or an alternative corrective action to demonstrate that FPI has addressed the concerns documented in this report and adjusted the performance metric for its job-sharing initiative so that it more directly quantifies FPI's efforts to employ more inmates.

2. **Unresolved.** BOP did not state whether it concurred with our recommendation that FPI establish organization-wide or business group targets for the job-sharing initiative, and reestablish performance metrics for responsible officials' performance work plans to incentive meeting those targets. BOP stated in its response that FPI continues to make excellent progress on its job-sharing initiative through nationwide telephone conferences and videoconferences; the issuance of written guidelines; and tracking the initiative through agency Strategic Plans and monthly and quarterly reporting. BOP's response also stated that although job-sharing performance measures and rating criteria are no longer included in responsible officials' performance work plans, FPI's job sharing data confirms that excellent progress has been made in increasing the number of inmates participating in job-sharing. BOP provided the following exhibit showing that in the third quarter of FY 2013, approximately 21 percent of its inmate employees worked part-time, a 57 percent improvement from FY 2012.

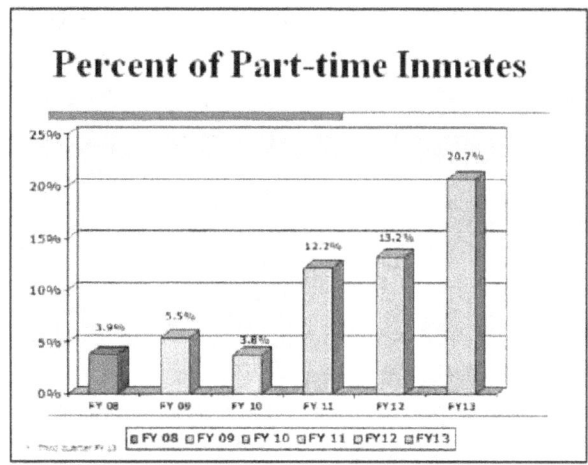

Source: BOP/FPI

BOP's response appears to indicate that FPI is still tracking its job-sharing progress using the data about part-time employees that our report found, on pages 18-19, to be unreliable and insufficient to provide an accurate reflection of the job-sharing initiative's success. (In our report and in this appendix, we use "part-time" and "half-time" interchangeably.) Specifically, FPI's method of counting half-time employees does not adequately distinguish between half-time jobs created through the job-sharing initiative, and half-time jobs created for other reasons, such as a factory that already operated half-shifts prior to the job-sharing initiative, full-time jobs that are converted to

39

half-time due to declining workload, and inmates whose work hours are half-time due to call-outs rather than as a result of job-sharing. For these reasons, we found that the job-sharing data FPI collected from September 2010 through March 2012 – data that appears to be reflected in the exhibit included in the BOP's response – to be significantly inaccurate.

In our judgment, an increase in the percentage of part-time inmate employees need not preclude FPI from establishing organization-wide or business group targets for the job-sharing initiative, or from maintaining performance targets and rating criteria for responsible officials. We believe that establishing organization-wide or business group targets and resuming the use of rating criteria for responsible officials would help incentivize continued job-sharing success and also enable FPI to better analyze its progress toward achieving performance expectations.

To resolve and close this recommendation, please provide evidence that FPI has established organization-wide or business group targets for the job-sharing initiative, and reestablished performance metrics for responsible officials' performance work plans to incentivize meeting those targets, or evidence of an alternative corrective action that sufficiently addresses this recommendation.

3. **Unresolved.** BOP did not concur with our recommendation to finalize a policy to replace FPI's previous inmate employment goal with one that is better aligned with FPI's current operational and economic environment. BOP stated in its response that changes to the inmate employment goal should not be made at this time because it believes that FPI can make significant strides toward reaching its current employment goal by capitalizing on its new repatriation and Prison Industry Enhancement Certification Program authorities and through the implementation of employment initiatives, including job-sharing and hiring prioritizations. BOP's response also stated that FPI has achieved this goal in the past and does not want to lower its desired goal and expectations for the future.

While we appreciate BOP's desire to not want to lower its goals and expectations for FPI, BOP's response provides only a general explanation of why it believes FPI can achieve its existing 25 percent employment goal in the future. As described on page 25 of this report, in order to have met its 25 percent employment goal in June 2012, FPI would have needed to provide work for over 44,000 inmates, roughly three times as many inmates as FPI employed at that time and nearly double the highest employment level ever achieved by FPI. Moreover, using FPI's current definition of "eligible BOP inmate population," FPI has not met its 25 percent employment goal since 1989, and as of March 2013, FPI employed just 8 percent of the inmate population housed in BOP facilities. We also note that BOP's response appears to represent a departure from the sentiment FPI officials conveyed to the OIG during the course of our audit. Those officials told the OIG that due to the continued rise in the eligible inmate population, among other factors, the 25 percent employment goal is no longer representative of current conditions, and that they were developing a proposal for a new goal that would be more consistent with the Department's commitment to performance-based management and reflective of FPI's available resources and evolving operational and economic environment.

To resolve and close this recommendation, please either provide a finalized policy to replace FPI's previous inmate employment goal with one that is better aligned with FPI's current operational and economic environment, or provide a detailed performance-based management plan for FPI that demonstrates how the 25 percent goal is attainable going forward.

4.   **Unresolved.** BOP did not state whether it concurred with our recommendation that FPI establish internal control procedures to ensure that it no longer considers for hire or employs aliens who have received a final order of deportation, exclusion, or removal, when doing so is prohibited by law, regulation, or policy. BOP stated in its response that FPI is currently in compliance with Program Statement 8120.02 and 28 C.F.R. § 345.35(a), and that it has confirmed that the only inmates working for FPI who have received a final deportation order are those who qualify for a policy exception, and cannot be removed from the U.S. because the designated country of removal will not allow them to return. BOP further stated that FPI has provided the field with guidance on BOP/FPI policy in Program Statement 8120.02, that FPI intends to remind managers of this requirement during the next management video conference, and that this information will be included in the monthly operational reports for all factories.

BOP's response did not provide enough information about the internal control procedures FPI has established to demonstrate that they are sufficient to ensure that FPI no longer hires or employs aliens in contravention of law, regulation, or policy.

To resolve and close this recommendation, please provide evidence demonstrating that FPI established internal control procedures sufficient to ensure that it no longer considers for hire or employs aliens who have received a final order of deportation, exclusion, or removal, when doing so is prohibited by law, regulation, or policy.

www.ingramcontent.com/pod-product-compliance
Lightning Source LLC
Chambersburg PA
CBHW081756280526
45789CB00008B/2872